FRANK ASCH

Water

Voyager Books • Harcourt, Inc.

Orlando   Austin   New York   San Diego   London

www.hmhco.com

First Voyager Books edition 2000
Voyager Books is a registered trademark of Harcourt, Inc.

The Library of Congress has catalogued the hardcover edition as follows:
Asch, Frank.
Water/Frank Asch.
p. cm.
1. Water—Juvenile literature. [1. Water.] I. Title. II. Series.
GB662.3.A83   1995   553.7—dc20   93-47967
ISBN 978-0-15-200189-6
ISBN 978-0-15-202348-5 pb

Printed in China
SCP 30 29 28
4500708054

The paintings in this book were done in watercolors,
acrylics, and colored pencils on Arches watercolor paper, series 500
The display type was set in Caxton book Italic. The text type was set in Goudy Old Style.
Color separations by Bright Arts, Ltd., Singapore
Printed and bound at RR Donnelley
Production supervision by Stanley Redfern
Designed by Lori J. McThomas

To Reid Antonacchio,
who loves to read

Water is rain.

Water is dew.

Water is ice and snow.

Water is high in the sky.

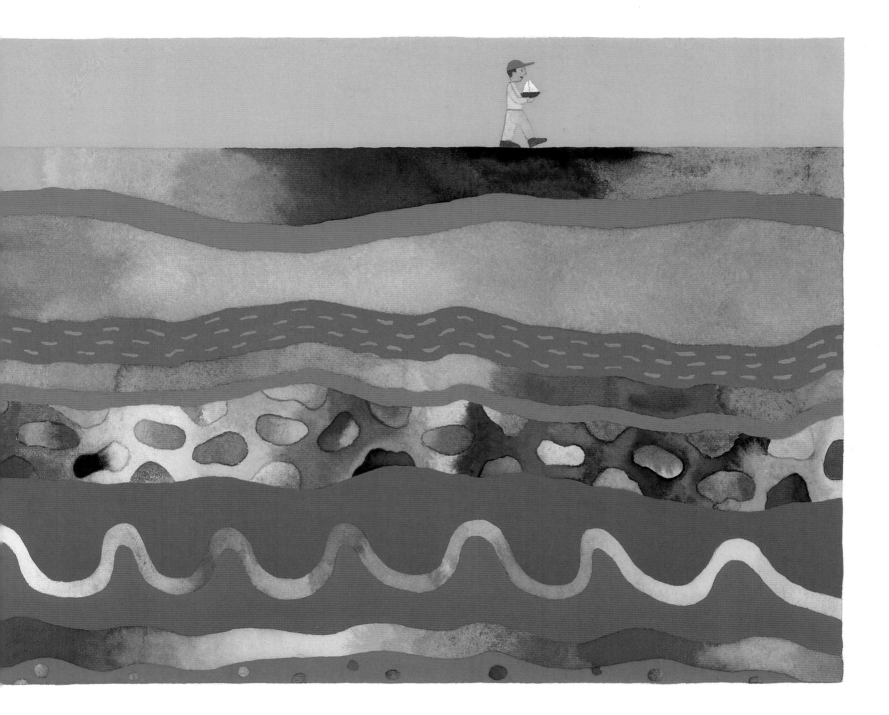

Water is deep in the earth.

Water is a tiny brook
growing bigger and bigger.

Water is a waterfall and mist.

Water is a small pond and a large lake.

Water is what fish *breathe . . .*

. . . and flowers *drink*.

Water is a salty tear.

Water is a flood.

Water is a long, winding river...

. . . flowing to the sea.